seven

years

seven years

poems on heartbreak and healing

by alyssa harmon

seven years copyright © 2022 by Alyssa Harmon. All rights reserved. Printed in the United States. No part of this book may be used or reproduced in any manner whatsoever without written permission except in the case of reprints in the context of reviews.

Alyssa Harmon Publishing.

www.alyssa-harmon.com

ISBN: 979-8-9868131-0-3

This book is a work of fiction. Names, characters, places, and incidents are products of the author's imagination or are used ficticuously. Any resemblance to actual events or locales or persons, living or dead, is entirely coincidental.

dedication

for aaron

table of contents

first year 1

late-night delusions 3
the road traveled too often 4
dog tag 5
green heart emoji 6
on a saturday morning 7
cereal boxes 8
fortune teller 9
when you fall in love with a writer 10
obvious 13
"why is kissing in the rain romantic?" 14
a car advertisement 15
you are on the fastest route 16
magnetar 17
leather-bound journals 18

second year 19

no label is still a label 21
boa constrictor 22
emptiness 23
mirrors 24
nephelococcygia 25
some fairytales don't have happy endings 26
april 22, 2016 27
light the way 28
"it's all fun and games until someone gets hurt" 29
memorial day 30
selenelion 31

table of contents (cont)

lacheism 32
a halloween nightmare 33
paint by number 34
it's what they don't tell you 35
two truths and a lie 36

third year **37**

red in the morning, sailor's warning 39
written in the stars 40
boreas: the bringer of cold, winter air 41
home for the holidays 42
no one talks about cleaning up after the fireworks ... 43
connecting two independent clauses 45
calidris 46
an imperfect palindrome 47
mathematics 48
consent 49
power lines 50
landmarks 51
you always hated him 52
it was supposed to be safe 53
you brought a rubik's cube on our road trip 54

fourth year **55**

kalopsia 57
headphones don't last forever 58
vibrations 59
permanent sunsets 60
double deal 61
local art 62

table of contents (cont)

60,000 miles 63
the doctor's office 64
monophobia 65
money can't buy happiness 66
you can't relight a used match 67
don't unpack for a short stay 68
anchors 69
why haircuts come after breakups 70

fifth year **71**

thymesis 73
some things never change 77
i miss you 78
it still fits 79
everyone says goodbye 80
we were lightning 81
the morning crossword puzzle 82
cape cod, kettle cooked chips 83
they all fall down 84
drinking games 85
cut the bullshit 86

sixth year **87**

geometry 89
april 10, 2018 90
do you feel like you can't trust anyone? 91
under construction 92
pieces of us 94
tsundoku 95
to the girl who loves him next 96

table of contents (cont)

typos...97
i lost you and found him................................98
is this okay?...99

seventh year.. 101

closer..103
why don't you write happy poems?...........104
types of guys not to fall in love with........105
favorite shade of lipstick.............................106
why they name hurricanes after people....107
"please don't write about me"...................108
the naked eye...109
puzzle pieces..110
it's because of him......................................111
a guided meditation...................................112
2023..114

"'i learned that writing is the consolation prize you are given when you don't get the thing you want the most.'"

-lang leav, *sad girls*

first year

late-night delusions

i don't remember much from that night,
but i do remember your scent—
how it smelled like unfulfilled desire,
tainted with a hint of late-night delusions.
the taste of cold stone and cough drops,
delight and desolation wrapped into one,
an alluring appetizer of contentment.

the road traveled too often

follow the trail of clothes

from the door to the bed;

follow the road called

"i swear we're just friends."

dog tag

the only thing

between us

was the dog tag

hanging from my neck,

its cold metal

warmed between

our naked chests.

green heart emoji

a flickering beacon in an unlit world,

a worn and faded welcome mat,

the faint smell of home that's always there

but never noticed until after you're gone

for a while.

on a saturday morning

let's watch the lightning dance across the naked white walls

while lying in bed watching 1990s spider-man cartoons.

legs as tangled as my unbrushed hair,

somnolent neck and forehead kisses.

"i'll always love you," the tv murmurs

as the rain taps morse code on the window:

"wake up."

cereal boxes

trying to find the right partner

is like trying to pick out the

cereal box that has

the perfect toy inside.

fortune teller

every moment i experience déjà vu

i try to see further into the future

and try to find out if i end up

with you.

alyssa harmon

when you fall in love with a writer

he'll write about

the way the light-colored

birthmark on her lower stomach

changed shapes whenever

she laughed at her own jokes.

how he never wanted

her to get out of bed

because he liked to count

the freckles on her naked face

before she hid them with makeup for the day.

the teasing smile on her face

as she danced in the messy kitchen

to the quick rhythm of latin music.

seven years

how she would always eat
the orange and yellow starbursts
because she didn't want those colors
to feel unloved.

the way her lips always
tasted of burt's bees wild
cherry lip balm.

the time she saved an ant
on a leaf in the pool,
when she scooped the spider
onto her shoe and let it outside.

the way her hair smelled like
redken diamond oil after a
steaming, late night,
hour-long shower.

how her hair would only be

in a messy bun if

she had a good idea,

and he'll write about how

he could never find someone else

like her.

obvious

one night i asked you

why you called me love

and let's be honest,

i knew the answer,

i just wanted to hear

you say it

one

        more

                time.

alyssa harmon

"why is kissing in the rain romantic?"

have you ever experienced

a floridian afternoon thunderstorm?

all the exciting buildup—

mysterious dark clouds,

a steamy atmosphere,

the petrichor perfume,

powerful gusts of wind,

the first few drops of rain

teasing what's to come—

until eventually the clouds can't take it anymore

and relinquish all their control

for just a few moments of bliss

before everything returns back

to normal,

and everyone pretends

like nothing happened.

a car advertisement

1997 jeep wrangler:

62,416 miles

manual transmission

    (that's why he won't hold your hand)

gas meter not very reliable

    (or maybe it was just his poor judgment)

cool a/c for the sticky florida summers

removable soft top for unplanned drives in storms

a loud engine to fill the heavy silences

one too many nights spent in the backseat

you are on the fastest route

i never understood why
people drive under
the speed limit on the highway
until you were riding shotgun.

magnetar

one night while we laid on top of the car, watching the stars,

you said we were like magnets

and that's why we were so attracted to each other,

but i say we are rare magnetars;

the remains of something magnificent

that couldn't continue, with a collapsed core,

we burned and turned maroon before exploding

on a cosmic level,

becoming the strongest magnet in the galaxy

and now we have power,

the kind of power that can tear planets

apart.

leather-bound journals

"you're like one of those leather-bound journals with a lock on it.

once you open it up and read a little bit,

you finally understand why it's locked."

-you never stopped searching for the key

second year

no label is still a label

when i type your address into google maps
a blue screen popped up to ask
if i go there often and
if so, what did i want it to
call the destination?
so i typed:

"he doesn't like labels."

boa constrictor

your arms were the place i

felt safest

until you kissed me.

emptiness

at the end of the night

we were both as empty

as that dimly lit marina

parking lot we spent the night in.

mirrors

i was the ocean

and you were the sky.

you took away my color

and i became just a

mirror of

you.

nephelococcygia

    the act of seeking and finding shapes in clouds

you say

it is rare for two people to see

the same image in clouds.

we see each other's hands

drifting away in the wind and

pretend the blue sky

is not dividing us.

some fairytales don't have happy endings

i was thrown out to the world with

no map or directions,

so i found myself

leaving a trail of clothes like breadcrumbs

back to his front door.

but the birds devoured it in the middle of the night

and i wandered around

trying to find my way home

starving,

cold,

looking for anything, anyone, to help me survive

when i stumbled upon his house,

he offered me what i wanted:

a chance to feel needed again.

april 22, 2016

sometimes you were my sandbar

saving me when my feet couldn't

find the bottom,

but most times you were the wave that stole

all the sand from underneath me.

light the way

we were distorted moonlight on choppy waves

providing a yellow brick exit,

we were sunlight flickering through

the leaves of the trees

casting shadows.

we were always broken, fragmented,

enjoying the brief moments of happiness

when we had them.

seven years

"it's all fun and games until someone gets hurt"

i never thought that

the phrase my mom drilled into

my head would be my last thought

before falling asleep

in your bed.

memorial day

gold trophies covered in dust on the top of the bookshelf,

faded ribbons and medals hung off colored push pins,

military memorabilia scattered like spider webs across the desk,

the empty piñata dangling from the ceiling,

an open window with tattered curtains blowing in the breeze,

a door that won't stay shut.

selenelion

> *"a phenomenon that occurs when the sun and moon are 180 degrees apart in the sky at the same time"*

in a bed that he abandoned in the middle of the night,

his two cats curled up, warming my bare feet

as if they knew how lonely

waking up alone would be while

an ombre of pastels developed

on the horizon of the bay,

even the moon stayed long enough

to make sure the sun was okay.

lacheism

english, the desire to be struck by a disaster

you know you're fucked

when you find peace in something so

poetic yet so

violent and damaging

like a rainbow in a hurricane, and

maybe that's why i ignored all the

dead end signs as we continued driving.

why i thought i could brave your storm

as i watched everyone else evacuate,

why i ignored the blaring sirens

as we spent the night in an abandoned house,

why i simply turned the fire alarms off

as you watched me turn into ashes

i watched the flames dance in your eyes.

a halloween nightmare

empty reese's and snickers wrappers scattered like regret on the living room floor a red bandana a denim button down and a rank-less military jacket tossed on the couch the gentle glow of old reruns of fresh prince of belair canvas the room him asleep on the other couch but you are always the one awake wondering how the hell you ended up in this situation you want to go to sleep but don't want to wake him because he looks so peaceful and you think his sleep matters more than the insomnia and chaos he left behind

on a halloween night

paint by number

1. gray. the blow-up air mattress in the echoing room.
2. white. the color of the pillow we were sharing.
3. brown. the blanket half thrown off the mattress.
4. red. the duffel bag that held all i thought i needed.
5. green. our clothes on the other side of the room.
6. blue. the color he made me feel.
7. black. the room after he closed the door.

it's what they don't tell you

they say

if you love someone

let them know,

but they don't warn you

what will happen

when he stares at the floor

and whispers *i'm sorry.*

two truths and a lie

i think you're pretty.

you'll be okay.

i want everything to do with you, and i only feel that for you.

third year

red in the morning, sailor's warning

the more beautiful the sunrise,

the worse the storm.

the morning after we met,

the sky was every color but blue.

written in the stars

no matter how much i search the sky

i can't find our names

hidden in the constellations,

yet i keep trying.

boreas: the bringer of cold, winter air

if you listen closely to the wind

it whispers over and over

"you already know how this ends."

alyssa harmon

home for the holidays

spending the holidays without you

is like being the only house

in the neighborhood

without colorful christmas lights

brightening up the neighborhood.

seven years

no one talks about cleaning up after the fireworks

"are you sure you know how to-"

"i think i know how to handle-"

right before it exploded in his hand

boom

everyone on the pier drinking champagne

the flash from cameras reflecting off their

2016 dollar store glasses and glittery cardboard top hats

boom

boom

he kisses you, saying he'll be right back,

you call his name as he runs towards his car

"what?" he stops and asks

"you have seventeen minutes!" you tap an imaginary watch

"romantic," his friend snickers and hands you a solo cup

as if they knew you'd need it to deal with

what was about to come next

alyssa harmon

>*boom*

>*boom*

>*boom*

when will you admit he's never coming back?

>*happy*

new year

connecting two independent clauses

she always used semicolons;

she was determined not to let

anything else good end.

calidris

i observed a baby sanderling

scurry towards the water

playing tag with the relentless waves

because he needed food

to survive,

and i thought, well,

maybe i shouldn't let go yet.

seven years

an imperfect palindrome

our relationship

mathematics

you said you were just splitting

your time and attention

between the two of us

but zero divided by two

is still

zero.

consent

the cool breeze

asking so politely

to see what's under her dress

the gust of angry wind

who thinks he's entitled to

the skin underneath.

power lines

our arrangement was no-strings-attached

but by the end

i was attached to so many

strings like a puppet, and

you were the master.

landmarks

the walgreens on the corner

but not on the corner of happy and healthy,

the corner of love and lost time;

the 7-11

where you knew to turn left to get back home

on the street called

"you're supposed to feel safe here";

the liquor store near his house

and the pothole filled back road--

you're lost,

but he won't help you find your way.

you always hated him

how dare he

love something you broke,

how dare he

take the time to pick up the pieces

you scattered on the ground

how dare he

stay, when you weren't man enough

to stick around.

seven years

it was supposed to be safe

you fell into him

the way butter sinks into fresh toast

all the aloe in the world

won't soothe the pain of him

and ever since, you've been searching

for something you lost

like trying to find the twist tie

that blends in with the granite countertop.

you brought a rubik's cube on our road trip

you were always so good at solving those damn puzzles,

and decided it would be fun to make me your own personal game.

so you mixed my whites with yellows

reds with oranges

my blues with greens.

redgreenbluefuckyellowwhiteorangeshit

i was an unaesthetic disaster and even

though you had the ability

to fix me you left me like that a challenge

for a rainy day if you got bored i tried

to peel the stickers off and rearrange

them but it still didn't feel right so you left

me to spend years figuring out the

algorithm to put myself back

    to

        ge

            ther

fourth year

kalopsia

> *greek, the delusion of things being more beautiful than they are*

you should delete the voicemails

accusing you of never being there

standing underneath the scalding shower

telling yourself that you'll get used to it

when he said i love you,

you didn't realize that it was april 1st

a journal filled with "i gave him the world, but

maybe i should've tried harder"

screaming at a dying flower because

it wouldn't grow fast enough,

but it didn't deprive itself of sunlight

walking into his bedroom but forgetting

what exactly you were looking for

gazing into a mirror that shows

how happy you could be without him.

headphones don't last forever

it started on march 1st

when you walked through that door

with that look on your face

and i ran to kiss you hello

and hug you because your

arms were my home,

but suddenly

i was given an eviction notice.

vibrations

you took off my glasses

so i wouldn't see you leave,

but i felt the earth

vibrate as you walked away.

permanent sunsets

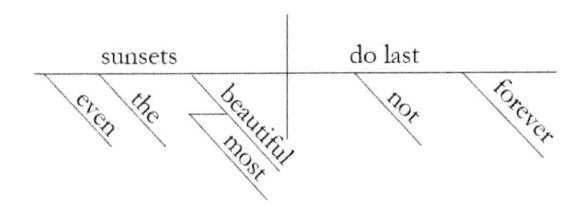

                    |
        sunsets | do last
    ───────────────────────────────
       \   \   \   \   \
      even the beautiful not   forever
              most

double deal

you said i was the one holding all the cards

but you were the one bribing the dealer

underneath the table.

local art

you left all your shit here

like i was supposed to make some

shrine out of it

and call it

what happens when you get attached.

but i'm the broken sculpture,

pieces scattered on the ground

this one's called

what happens when he decides

not to stick around.

60,000 miles

there are 60,000 miles

of blood vessels in a

human body and somehow

you managed to cause a car crash

on every single inch of mine.

the doctor's office

you can't keep running back to the people

who gave you the bruises

expecting them to kiss and heal your wounds.

monophobia

i promised to kill your spiders;

you promised to kill my bees -

together we could

conquer the world.

now there is a swarm of bees

outside of my house.

money can't buy happiness

your happiness was

a dime that you were

so proud of earning,

but he convinced you to trade

with him because

he had a nickel,

and he told you it was worth more

because it was a bigger coin.

seven years

you can't relight a used match

but what if it was a trick candle

what if we didn't blow hard enough

what if the flame never actually went out?

don't unpack for a short stay

all your baggage was perfectly packed

before you met him;

somehow it all fit

but now he's gone

and you can't zip your suitcase shut.

anchors

humans can't walk in a straight line

without a point of reference,

something to hold onto,

and ever since you left

there have been circles

permanently pressed into the carpet.

why haircuts come after breakups

in front of the cracked mirror,
scissors shake in her hands as
his voice echoes off the bathroom tile
"i love your hair that way."

fifth year

thymesis

greek, memory

1.

you had green eyes

i had blue;

you liked her

when i liked you.

2.

we never got the timing right,

two cars that

passed the intersection

only a few seconds apart.

3.

you were my

favorite author because

you wrote our story,

but you couldn't write the ending.

4.

no one ever asks why

you get scared so easily why

you jump when a guy first touches you

or puts his arm around you.

5.

"it's okay,"

you whispered,

"it's just me."

maybe that was the problem.

6.

the doctor says,

"show me where it hurts,"

and you just stand there

with your arms spread out.

7.

107.3

i found myself

driving and listening to your

favorite radio station.

8.

before you left

you handed me

some tape and glue

and whispered, "good luck."

9.

i keep waiting for the phone to ring

or for you to show up at my door

saying the words

"i can't live without you anymore."

10.

most people only sleep

with one or two pillows; i sleep with

seven or eight because i need something

to fill up the bed's empty space.

11.

i like to take long showers

and let the soap,

water, and shampoo

wash away every single trace of you.

12.

they say that it takes twenty-one days

to break a bad habit.

well that can't be true because it's been

five years and i'm still in love with you.

some things never change

if someone put all the people i've loved

in the same room,

i'd still walk in and

search their faces

for yours.

i miss you

i don't remember when

we started saying "i love you"

it just seemed like the natural thing to do.

i do remember when

you said "i'm leaving you."

it still fits

if it doesn't smell like him anymore

is it okay to wear your ex's

blue american eagle sweatshirt

even if the white letters are fading

even if the sleeves are fraying

even if it's five years later?

everyone says goodbye

she cries a little when the tiny, old, blue, beat-up car that's been driving next to her for seventeen miles gets off on exit 24. no warning, save for a blinker at the last minute as he swerves all the way from the left lane to the exit.

we were lightning

did you know that
> lightning is caused by
>> the negative particles
>>> (the glass is always half empty)
>>>> sinking to the bottom
>>>>> (of the bottle)
>>> the positive particles react
>> (invite him over to "just talk")
> and a spark occurs

(it was a one-night fling)
> just like that
>> (he knew)
>>> it disappears.

alyssa harmon

the morning crossword puzzle

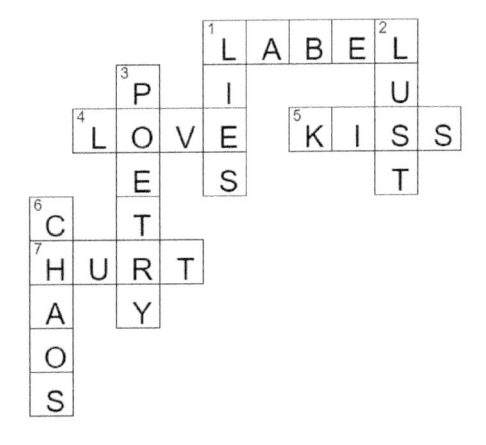

```
        L A B E L
      P   I     U
    L O V E   K I S S
      E   S     T
    C   T
    H U R T
    A   Y
    O
    S
```

across

1. what you refused to give us

4. the only reason i stayed

5. the beginning of our end

7. what you did to me

down

1. what you used to get me into your bed

2. why you wanted me

3. how to cope with the loss of you

6. what we created

seven years

cape cod, kettle cooked chips

my mom always packs a salad with

chopped up chicken, peppers, mushrooms, onions, shredded cheese, eggs,

and a ziploc bag full of cape cod kettle cooked chips for my dad

for work the next day. one day, i asked her why—

he's a grown man — can't he do it himself?

she told me that "we should do things

we don't want to do

for the people that we care about."

does that rule still apply to

the night my boyfriend convinced me

to join him in his bed?

they all fall down

hallelujah comes on
in the store; she
sinks to the
dirty ground and
cries like some-
one played jenga
with her feelings
and they just pulled
the wrong
                block.

drinking games

never have i ever

said i love you without

believing i meant it.

all my exes

lower one finger.

cut the bullshit

he said that it was better to have loved and

lost than to have never loved at all,

but the problem is he never

loved me.

sixth year

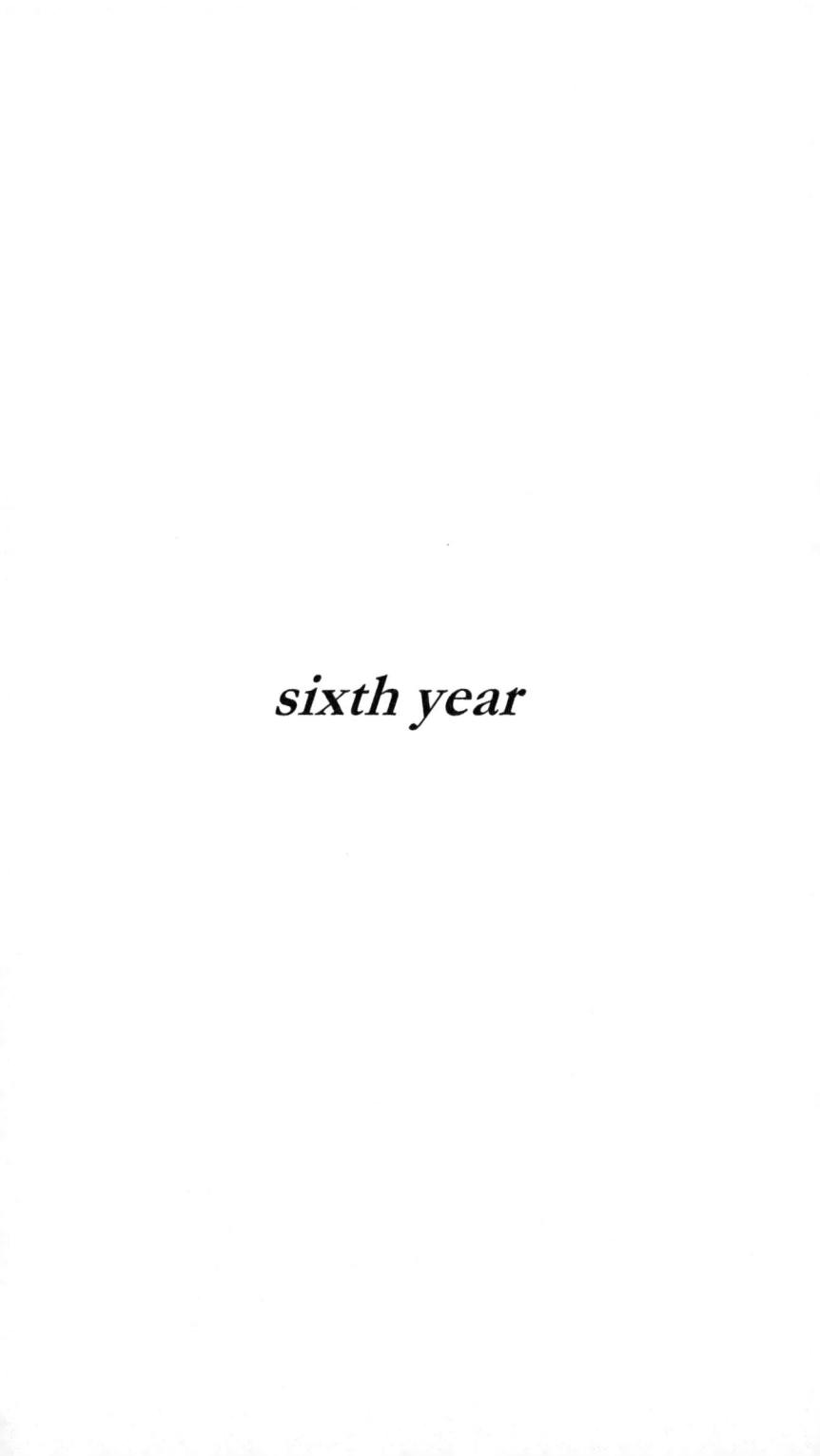

geometry

we were one of those toys—

the one cube with holes carved out

for the corresponding shapes.

but you had holes for squares, circles, and triangles,

and i was composed of hearts, stars, and crescent moons.

april 10, 2018

he asked me what i wanted most

out of my life and i said

happiness.

he thought it was cheesy and cliche

but i see it as you don't know what you have

until you've lost it.

do you feel like you can't trust anyone?

do you ever feel like the bird

who flies away when someone wanders by,

the lizard who scurries across the sidewalk

when he hears footsteps,

the crab that hides back in its hole

when it sees a shadow?

under construction

this house has been under construction

since 2016, and there is no end in sight.

so why would i ask you to live in this one

where when the rain falls,

it falls hard.

when the wind blows,

it takes everything with it.

when the earth slightly shakes,

the beams come crashing down.

why would i ask you to live in a house

that is on top of a gravesite knowing

that it will most definitely be haunted by

all kinds of ghosts when you move in?

there are many more unhaunted, safe, and stable

houses on the market.

so why would i ask you to live in this one?

pieces of us

please tell me our names are

still engraved on that metal pole

please tell me our i love you's

are still on the park bench in sharpie

please tell me at a least a part of us

made it.

tsundoku

> *japanese, stack of books that you have purchased but not yet read*

but you know she's bad at

closing chapters

she has a whole library at home,

yet she keeps re-reading the same book.

to the girl who loves him next

just be careful,

i'm not saying people never change,

i'm just saying i tried for two and a half

years to change him

and he never did.

typos

i love you

*i loved the idea of you

i lost you and found him

orion's belt was my favorite constellation

because it was the only one i could find

but one night someone showed me

that what i thought was orion was actually the big dipper -

the constellation i had been searching for

all along.

is this okay?

he asked me if this was okay

and if that was okay

and if i was sure i wanted to

because i was a little bit tipsy—

would i regret this in the morning?

and i said i wouldn't, but he asked

me again anyways to

make sure,

and i said,

yes.

my ex used to ask

if this was okay,

but it was after

telling me that this was

the last chance we would have,

so we better do it now. or

when he said he would never

pressure me but… or

when he whispered

"it's okay

it's just me" in my ear. or

when he told me if i didn't

he wouldn't stay with me-

remember the last time

i said no?

so i said,

yes.

seventh year

closer

objects in the mirror

are closer than they appear;

your healing and happiness

really aren't that far away,

you just have to let them catch up to you.

why don't you write happy poems?

writing poetry is the first aid kit
i keep underneath the bathroom sink.
writing poetry is the emergency room -
you don't go when you're healthy.
writing poetry is the pen and paper inside
of the in-case-of-emergency-break-glass.

types of guys not to fall in love with

"make the first move,"

"i'm not really looking for a relationship,"

"you knew what you were getting yourself into,"

"that's not a good enough excuse,"

"what did you want me to do to show that i cared,"

"this is your last chance."

favorite shade of lipstick

her favorite shade of lipstick

was the dark maroon color

called "it's time to move on."

why they name hurricanes after people

hurricane you-knew-it-would-be-a-beautiful-disaster

hurricane they-all-warned-you-but-you-didn't-listen

hurricane let's-face-it-he-was-lonely-and-so-were-you

hurricane they-were-right-you-need-to-love-yourself-first

"please don't write about me"

don't expect me to apologize

for how i've healed

after all,

"literature deserves an audience"

the naked eye

never apologize for seeing

the good in people even if

you have to use a microscope.

puzzle pieces

someone once told me that

people will push you away

if they were hurt before

and suddenly everything made sense.

it's because of him

you spend so much time

writing these poems

for him

despite the fact that he never

read them

but at the end of the day,

they're not for him,

they're for your healing

because of him.

a guided meditation

close your eyes.

notice your breathing.

the rapid rise and fall of your chest

against his,

fingertips read your goosebumps like braille

and it spells out "please stay."

notice your heavy breathing.

the way his kisses play connect the dots with the freckles on your arm,

and the final picture turns out to be a broken clock

be aware of your surroundings.

orion watches from the sky, wishing he could save you

the hum of the radio plays "how to love,"

the mosquitoes buzz in your ears, and if you listen closely

they whisper warnings.

take one last deep breath,

feel the pressure of his chest on yours disappear,

notice the gradual absence of his touch

notice the labyrinth you feel.

realize that one day you'll be okay again.

open your eyes.

2023

> *"every cell in your body is replaced after seven years" -
> one study claims*

seven more years

and maybe by then

my tongue will

erase your taste.

six more years and maybe

my chest will forget

the roughness of your lips.

five more years and maybe

the veins in my arms

won't recall which route

your fingers used to travel.

four more years

and maybe my heart

will forgive the bruises

seven years

it sustained

after you dropped it one too

many times because you

were always so bad at

catching things before

they hit the ground.

three more years and

maybe the dark circles

under my eyes will

fade away along

with the memory of

sleepless nights filled

with circular arguments.

two more years and

maybe my brain

will unstitch the sadness

you embroidered into

its memory.

one more year

and maybe then

i won't remember

you.

acknowledgements

writing the poems was easy; organizing them into a collection was the difficult part. i wouldn't have been able to do it without the support of friends like travis. thank you for agreeing to be my thesis advisor and help me workshop all these poems and put together a cohesive collection. you weren't afraid to push me to be the best writer i could be while also listening to my breakdowns in the library. you continue to take time out of your busy schedule to always help me and support my poetry, and this book wouldn't be what it is today without your help.

emma, thank you for reading all my poems and not being afraid to give me the truth. you helped me sharpen my talents and get me to where this book could be published. and i knew i could always count on you to help my change all my passive verbs into active ones.

thank you to eric for being one of my biggest supporters from day one. you've always been there to read my new work, help with old projects, and give me confidence in my art. more importantly, you reminded me to never let anyone take away the power of my words, and i will never forget that.

thank you to all my professors who helped me perfect my craft and watched me grow as a writer and a poet. from dr. conner who let me work on every poetic project possible, to professor peterson who taught my first creative writing class, to dr. armstrong who was on my thesis committee, and to dr. smith who gave me the space to work on my poetic thesis.

from a young age, my parents were also supportive of my writing. they've listened to me talk about the different books and projects that i wanted to write, and they supported me through my career and education in english. matthew, thank you for saving the day and helping with the cover, and, daniel, thank you for supporting my instagram page from day one.

thank you to sierra, natalie, tim, emily, sam, sara, jon, albert, derek, and everyone else who have helped me publish this book in some capacity. there are too many to name, but just know that this book is for you too.

aaron, you're the one who showed me that it was okay to love again. you supported me through this entire journey, listening to me talk about this project and celebrating every new milestone, no matter how small, and you were my biggest cheerleader throughout the whole process. you don't know how much your support means.

lastly, this book wouldn't even be here if it wasn't for all my fans. i've made so many connections through the poetry community, and you all encouraged me to put my work out there. when poetry helped me get through difficult times, i knew i wanted to give back to the community and help someone else, and you guys are helping me do just that. thank you. if you enjoyed this book, please leave a review on amazon or goodreads so others can enjoy it as well!

first appeared in

"lacheism" first appeared in The *Merrimack Review*.

"landmarks" and "local art" first appeared in *Papercut Literary Journal*.

"2023" first appeared in *Odet Journal, Volume 3*.

"the wind," now titled "consent," first appeared in *Minerva Rising*.

"a car advertisement," "everyone says goodbye," and "you are on the fastest route," first appeared in *Politics Letter: Car Poems*.

"dog tag" and "no label is still a label" first appeared in *30 N*.

"a guided meditation" and "why they name hurricanes after people" first appeared in *Semiotics - an Anthology on Modern Love, Sexuality, and Desire*.

"when you fall in love with a writer" first appeared in *Pinnacle Anthology*.

"they all fall down" first appeared in *Spire Light*.

"nephelococcygia" first appeared in *The Blue Bird Word*.

"late night delusions" first appeared in *Thread Literary Inquiry* and *Shaking the Sheets Magazine*.

"we were lightning" first appeared in *Independent Variable*.

about the author

seven years is alyssa harmon's debut poetry collection. she graduated with her bachelor's in english writing studies from the university of south florida, st. petersburg, and is working on her master's in creative writing from the university of west florida. she writes poems based on her life experiences and will continue to write and share her words with the world. while this is her first book, she hopes to publish more that touch on subjects of mental health, healing, and the beauty of life. when she's not writing poetry, you can find her reading a good book, swimming laps in the pool, or traveling to new countries. to find more of her poetry, you can connect with her on instagram @alyssa_harmon_ or alyssa-harmon.com.

Printed in Great Britain
by Amazon